Between
You and I

a little book of $\underset{\wedge}{\overset{bad}{}}$ *english*

Between You and I

a little book of bad english

(with "bad" inserted above "english" and "little" and "english" underlined)

James Cochrane

Introduced by John Humphrys

SOURCEBOOKS, INC.
NAPERVILLE, ILLINOIS

Published by Sourcebooks, Inc.
P.O. Box 4410, Naperville, Illinois 60567-4410
(630) 961-3900
FAX: (630) 961-2168
www.sourcebooks.com

Library of Congress Cataloging-in-Publication Data
Cochrane, James.
  Between you and I : a little book of bad English / James Cochrane ;
introduced by John Humphrys.
      p. cm.
  Originally published: Cambridge, UK : Icon, 2003.
  (alk. paper)
  1. English language--Usage--Handbooks, manuals, etc. 2. English
language--Errors of usage--Handboooks, manuals, etc. I. Title.

PE1460.C55 2005
428--dc22

2004028667

Printed and bound in the United States of America
QW 10 9 8 7 6 5 4 3

Author's Preface

Between You and I is a book about Bad English. It is not about four-letter words or slang or split infinitives or ending a sentence with a preposition. It is not written from any inclination to be purist in the sense of proposing that change is to be resisted at all costs; on the contrary, not only is change inevitable but the constant renewal and enlargement of our wonderful language is generally to be welcomed rather than not. The kind of Bad English I was concerned with in compiling it is rarely to be found either in well-educated or in uneducated speech and writing, both of which have their strengths and weaknesses. It is a particular form of debasement which derives at least in part from what might be called the "half-educated" use of the language. Many of the words and phrases I included are, like the phrase that gives the book its title, spoken and written by people in the belief that they are more "correct" than the English they would have spoken naturally. Others are expressions from learned or technical discourse, often Latin or Greek by derivation, used—at best unnecessarily, at worst wrongly—in preference to humbler, common expressions with the same meaning: "epicenter," "criteria," and "discrete" spring to mind as examples. Others still are clichés used mindlessly; Simon Hoggart, in his review of the first edition of *Between You and I*, quoted the British health minister who told the House of Commons: "We are rolling out fresh fruit in primary schools." Almost invariably the examples come from people who ought to know better: broadcasters, particularly on BBC radio stations, journalists on the "quality" newspapers,

James Cochrane

politicians, public figures of all kinds, and, sadly, many teachers in both schools and universities, victims themselves, perhaps, of primary education in the "progressive" 1960s and 70s. Fortunately, this can be a "Little Book," because the most common examples of this kind of Bad English are still relatively few. As a result it can be read in only an hour or two. During that time, many readers may be surprised to find that much of what they thought was "bad" English is in fact perfectly good, and that what they have been led to think of as "good" English is sometimes ignorant, dishonest, or plain stupid. The first edition of *Between You and I* aroused the ire of Professor Terry Eagleton, who reviewed it in the *Irish Times* and hesitated for some time before deciding that the author was not a "quasi-fascist" but "just an old-fashioned English snob." (I'm actually an old-fashioned Scot; whether I'm also a snob I leave it to the reader to decide.) Other reviewers were much kinder, and many readers took the trouble to write to say how much they had enjoyed the book and how grateful they were to see so many of their own favorite bugbears denounced in print. Most of them, unlike the sternly Marxist Professor Eagleton, also managed to recognize a vein of humor running through the book. I am grateful to them for their kind words and for their suggestions about possible additional entries, some of which they will find in the pages that follow.

James Cochrane, May 2004

James Cochrane

Foreword

The story is told in journalistic circles of a crowd of journalists gathered outside the house of a very important man, all of them waiting for a very important announcement. The great man's butler came to the door, drew breath, and bellowed: "Would the press go around to the tradesman's entrance and will the gentleman from the *Times* please come with me!"

Ah, those were the days: the days when the *Times of London* was not just a newspaper but an institution. Pompous, stuffy, and old-fashioned it might have been, but it was respected throughout the world for its high standards. It was the newspaper of record. When the *Times* spoke, the world took note.

It got things right.

So when, a few years ago, I was asked to write my first column for the *Times*, I was flattered and agreed immediately. On the morning of publication I opened my copy. The headline above one of the stories on my page read: "Work Comes Second For Tony And I." In case you did not know, newspaper headlines are written not by the contributors but by sub-editors.

I was shocked. That a sub on the *Times* should commit such a howler was beyond belief. It was time, perhaps, to give up and accept that the battle for good English had been lost. It was all over. But then the letters began to arrive: a trickle that became a torrent. The readers were as shocked as I had been. And that reassured me. There are still many people out there who care enough for the English language to register their protest when they see it being desecrated. Many battles have been lost, but the war is not yet over.

James Cochrane

Perhaps it should be. Perhaps those of us who recoil at the incorrect use of "I" in a great newspaper are pedants. There is, after all, a danger that if we old fogies have our way the language will be treated as though it were a precious artifact in a museum. It will be kept carefully guarded day and night, protected from potential vandals. No one must be allowed to touch.

The French are a bit like that. The French Academy is the unchallengeable authority. It issues edicts about what may and may not be said and written. It strives to purge the sacred French language of any foreign—especially English—words that might defile its purity. It fails—and so it should.

Like any other organism, language changes. It lives in the real world and gets knocked around from time to time. It adapts in order to survive. Look up almost any word in the *Oxford English Dictionary* and you can follow the journey that it has taken over the centuries, changing its precise meaning as it twists and turns with the passing of time. Often its present meaning bears little relationship to its original one. It is silly to imagine that this evolution can be halted. It is even sillier to try.

But that is different from hoisting the white flag and surrendering to linguistic anarchy. A degree of discipline is not a constraint; it is a liberation. The more clearly we are able to express ourselves, the less room there is for ambiguity. The more elaborate and the more precise our vocabulary, the greater the scope for thought and expression. Language is about subtlety and nuance. It is powerful and it is potent. We can woo with words and we can wound. Despots fear the words of the articulate opponent. Successful revolutions are achieved with words as much as with weapons.

That is why Big Brother in George Orwell's *Nineteen Eighty-Four* had teams of workers endlessly removing words from the

James Cochrane

dictionary. Ultimately there would be no free expression, no way to express dissent. Utter obedience to totalitarian authority would be the only option.

When words with wholly distinct meanings become synonymous with each other—flaunt and flout, for instance—we begin to lose the capacity for discriminated expression. When we are cavalier about where we place the word "only" in a sentence we risk destroying its meaning. James Cochrane nicely illustrates that with his comic quotation from Marghanita Laski.

All this matters more in written than in spoken English. I have always felt it a little unfair for British parliamentary sketch writers to mock Deputy Prime Minister John Prescott by reproducing his garbled sentences verbatim in print. It might be difficult to follow him on the page, but he is capable of making a powerful speech. His audiences may not follow every point in his argument, but they know exactly what he means. I once saw him sway an audience at a Labour Party conference and win a crucially important vote that had been thought lost. He spoke from the heart and not the head and there is nothing wrong with that. But the writer does not have that license.

Flowery language from the pen of a poet is one thing; written English as a means of everyday communication is another. It should be plain and simple and accurate. It should use no more words than are needed to do the job and they should be the right words. We all have our own pet peeves. One of mine is the relatively recent and altogether hideous "met up with." I have offered a bottle of the best bubbly to anyone who can explain how that differs from "met." The bottle sits in my office to this day. I am with our postwar prime minister, Clement Attlee, on this. It was said of him that he would never use one word when none would do.

Then there is the tendency to use nouns as verbs. "Impact" is a good (by which I

James Cochrane

mean bad) example. Sadly, it has now entered the category of James Cochrane's "Lost Causes." They keep coming. "Fast track" was bad enough when it was overused as a noun. It is unspeakable as a verb.

This sort of thing flattens the language and destroys its vitality. "Disinterested" is an excellent word with a precise meaning. Now that it is used interchangeably with "uninterested" by those who should know better, its meaning has been destroyed. It is sad to lose a good word.

This is all of a piece with our lazy acceptance of jargon, using words for merely instrumental purposes rather than for genuine expression. It is not new—Orwell made the point in his classic essay "Politics and the English Language." Political speeches, he said, "consist less and less of words chosen for the sake of their meaning and more of phrases tacked together like the sections of a prefabricated hen-house."

Politicians have a lot to answer for, but

the real villains are businesspeople. Management-speak has been infiltrated into our lives, a loathsome serpent crawling into our bed at night and choking the life out of our language. It is an outrage that the phrase "human resources" was not strangled at birth. I hate it for its ugliness and its sloppiness. A moment's thought tells you that resources are exploited, used up, squeezed for every last drop of value, and then replaced. Are we really meant to regard human beings in that light? It seems we are. Or perhaps the vandals who created the phrase think that shortening it to "HR" erases the guilt. It does not.

Less offensive, but equally dreary, is all the mumbojumbo surrounding "delivering objectives" by "thinking outside the box" or "pushing the envelope" by "building on best practice." What does it all mean? I doubt that anyone really knows, least of all the people who use it. They tend to be middle managers striving to impress their bosses or,

James Cochrane

possibly, each other. The people at the top, in my experience, tend to communicate clearly. Maybe that's why they made it to the top in the first place. Lazy use of language suggests lazy thinking.

This hen-house language might not matter if it were confined to the business world. But it has escaped, like some malign virus, and is infecting us all. I would love to claim that the BBC, with its proud history of championing good English, is fighting back. Sadly, it is not. We have been suborned. A colleague of mine interviewed a young man who was applying for a job in his department. He asked him what he had been doing in the few months since he left Cambridge University. He was told: "Proactively networking."

He should have had him thrown out of the building on the spot or, better still, publicly executed, his body left to hang in the lobby of Television Center as a warning to others. Instead he gave him the job. The young man is now, I have no doubt, a middle manager telling his colleagues how he can "progress" his latest challenge—or some such nonsense.

There are so many threats to the survival of good, plain English that it is not easy to be optimistic. Email has a great deal to answer for. Punctuation is no longer required and verbs are abandoned with the speed of a striptease artiste late for her next performance. Text messaging is worse—much worse. Yet I have seen it suggested that students be allowed to use "texting" abbreviations in examinations. Ultimately, no doubt, we shall communicate with a series of grunts—and the evolutionary wheel will have turned full circle.

Happily, there are people like James Cochrane still prepared to fight the good fight. His subtitle is *A Little Book of Bad English*. There is a lot in it for a little book. Mr. Cochrane acknowledges that English is a living language and must change. But it

James Cochrane

must also be protected. We will all recognize many of his examples and have many more of our own. There is infinite scope for an infinite number of future editions.

John Humphrys, 2003

Between You and I

a little book of ₍bad₎ english

abrogate, arrogate A letter about the International War Crimes Tribunal in the *Guardian* newspapers on April 11, 2003, stated that powerful nations had "*Abrogated* to themselves the decision as to whether or not to recognize it" (italics added). Four days later, to its credit, the *Guardian* printed a correction: the word should have been *arrogated*.

To *abrogate* is to cancel, repeal, revoke.

To *arrogate* is to lay claim to something (normally an authority, a right, a position) without justification. The adjective is *arrogant*.

adverse, averse These two words are easily confused but should not be. *Adverse* means "unfavorable, hostile, harmful," as in "*adverse* weather conditions," "an *adverse* reaction," "*adverse* effects."

Averse can refer only to the inclinations of a person and means "disinclined, reluctant." It stems from Latin words meaning "turned from," and for that reason it was once correct English to say *averse from*; *averse to* is now much more usual.

agenda "Today's *agenda* is dauntingly long."

This looks at first sight like a Lost Cause. *Agenda* used to be a Latin gerundive plural, meaning "things requiring to be done," and on the face of it should be followed by a plural verb. But since no one nowadays admits to having only a singular *agendum* and since *agenda* has come to mean "a list of things requiring to be done or discussed" it is not really surprising that *agenda* has become a singular noun whose plural is *agendas*.

But see also REFERENDUM.

alibi Properly used, this is a legal term for a plea that when a crime was committed the accused was somewhere else, *alibi* being a Latin word meaning "elsewhere." The word is often used as if it meant simply "an excuse, a pretext" but should not be.

alternate, alternative *Alternate* can be a verb or an adjective conveying the idea of two things being done by turns, as in "The special service takes place on *alternate* Tuesdays" or "To build the wall he used layers of brick *alternated* with flint and mortar."

Alternative originally meant "the other of two" but it is now perfectly acceptable for it to mean a choice from among two or more things, courses of action, etc. Since the 1960s it has been used to mean "other than the traditional or the orthodox," as in "*alternative* medicine" or "the *alternative* society."

In the US, *alternate* is often found where British English would use *alternative*; e.g., as an adjective—the Book of the Month Club offers "*alternate* selections"—or as a noun for a substitute player in sports or a reserve juror.

amount, number *Amount* should normally be used with nouns that have no plural, e.g., *confusion*, *flattery*, *money*, *timber;* whereas *number* is used with nouns that have plurals, e.g., *children*, *weapons*, *problems*, *bills*. The use of *amount* where *number* would normally be used is acceptable if the plural noun that follows is viewed as an aggregate, as in "She noticed the amount of peas he was piling on his plate," where the peas are seen as a pile rather than actually counted, but too often it is used in this way with no justification whatsoever.

See also LESS AND FEWER.

Apostrophe, grocer's The term is used to describe the practice of forming the plural of a noun by the addition of an *apostrophe* followed by *s*, as in *potato's*, *banana's*, etc.

This is a little unfair to grocers, since they are by no means the only culprits, and the practice has spread to trades and even professions whose practitioners certainly ought to know better, e.g., journalists, lawyers, and real-estate agents.

The apostrophe is correctly used to express the possessive form of a noun ("the cat's whiskers") or to indicate that a letter has been omitted in a contraction such as "don't," "haven't," "isn't," etc. But note that pronouns do not need an apostrophe in their possessive form; hence the possessive form of *it* is *its*; the contracted form of *it is* is *it's*.

An apostrophe followed by *s* should be used for the possessive case in personal names except in cases where the resulting sound is unacceptably odd because, for example, there is an internal *s* in a name also ending with that letter; hence *Lucy's*, *James's*, *Dickens's*, but *Moses'*, *Ulysses'*, *Jesus'*.

Since most plurals end with an *s*, no further *s* is added to form the possessive, hence "the neighbors' children," "a cats' chorus." Where a plural noun is formed other than by adding an *s*, for example, *children*, *men*, an *s* is added, and the correct possessive form is, e.g., *children's* and *men's*. But the placing of the apostrophe in such words seems to be beyond the competence of many, even those who ought to know better, such as under-graduates of a certain Cambridge University college, who were recently observed sporting rowing shirts emblazoned with "Magdalene Boat Club *Mens'* Novice Squad 2002."

as and like Nowadays so many people say "It looks *like* it's going to rain" rather than "It looks *as if* it's going to rain" that this must probably be deemed a Lost Cause. It is also unlikely that people are going to be per-suaded to give up "It feels *like* I'm falling in love" in favor of "It feels *as if* I'm falling in love." However, the distinction between *like* and *as* is worth preserving in the name of both clarity and common sense.

James Cochrane

Consider the following sentences:

"*Like* tape recorders, people can now use this machine to copy CDs for little more than the cost of a blank disc." (Heard on BBC Radio 4.)

"*Like* all journeys in this country, it is almost impossible to travel anywhere with any confidence that you will arrive within a day of your anticipated time." (Jeremy Paxman in *Spectator* magazine, November 9, 2002.)

"*Like* 1991, most of the people of Basra are hoping for liberation from the regime in Baghdad." (BBC Radio 4 reporter during the war in Iraq.)

In the case of the first of these sentences, it should be evident that "people" are not "*like* tape recorders" and that the speaker should have said "*As* with tape recorders." In the same way, Jeremy Paxman would have been better to write, "*As* with all journeys in this country," and the BBC reporter on Iraq to have said, "*As* in 1991..."

The mistaken usage sometimes goes in the opposite direction, as in this example from BBC Radio 3: "*As* my other selections this morning, this two-CD album is available at mid-price," where it would have been logical as well as correct to say, "*Like* my other selections."

The grammatical rule is that *like* should be used before nouns (including personal names), noun phrases, and pronouns and *as* should be used before adverbs and prepositions ("*as* previously," "*as* in," "*as* with," etc.), but it is important also to be clear about what is being compared with what, as for example in the case of "*like* tape recorders" above.

as far as ... If we choose to start with this form of words it is necessary to complete it at some point by saying ... *is/are concerned*, as in "*As far as* my own opinions on the matter *are concerned* ..." or simply ... *goes*, as in "*As far as* that *goes*." To say something like "*As far as* our team's chances this season, I'm not holding my breath" is lazy and uneducated.

bacterium This is the singular form. *Bacteria* is the plural, but is so often used as a singular noun even in broadsheet newspapers that it is in danger of becoming a Lost Cause. The distinction seems worth preserving, if only in serious medical and scientific discourse.

basis, on a ... It can hardly ever be necessary to use this formula—as in *on a daily basis* or *on a regular basis*, rather than simply *daily* or *regularly*—unless it is to make a mock of a particular kind of pompous or bureaucratic discourse.

begging the question This is a term in logic

denoting a statement that proposes a conclusion based on a premise that has not been proved and that therefore *begs the question:* what is the evidence for that claim you slipped into what you've just said? An example might be: "Cows must be more intelligent than cats because their heads are bigger," which makes an assumption that *begs* to be challenged: namely that intelligence is directly linked to head size.

The phrase *begs the question* is occasionally used correctly in this way, but much more often it is used as if it meant simply *raises* or *leads to* a question, as in "Duffy's performance in last Saturday's game *begs the question* how much longer he can remain on the team." In this sentence, *raises the question* would have conveyed the speaker's meaning perfectly well, without devaluing a useful, if rather technical, expression.

behalf of, on This phrase means, or should mean, either "in the interest or for the benefit of" or "as the agent, spokesman, or representative of," as in "I want to thank you *on behalf of* the whole family." It is a serious mistake to use it in place of *on the part of* or to use *behalf* as a substitute for *part*, as in "That was a bad move *on your behalf*."

between…to This is an odd and infuriating use of the word *between*, which is normally and correctly used to signify a distinction or a difference, an interval between two points, or a relationship between two parties: we talk of the distance *between* London *and* Paris or the friendship *between* David *and* Jonathan. We talk about the difference *between* chalk *and* cheese.

In other words, when we are talking about two different things or points or parties *between* is invariably followed by *and*. Yet how often do we hear a weather forecaster talk of "temperatures *between* twenty *to* twenty-five degrees" or see notices announcing that "hours are *between* nine a.m.–five p.m."?

The correct and simple way to express ranges of time or distance or temperature is of course "*from...to*" and it is hard to find a reason for its not being used in these examples other than plain stupidity.

between you and I *Between*, *from,* and *to* are prepositions and take the accusative form of the noun. Even the many people who are unaware of this basic grammatical rule would not dream of saying "The distance *between we and* that hill" or "*From I to you*" or "*To I and* my wife." Yet all too often nowadays we find people saying, or even writing, "*Between you and I*" or "*From the wife and I*" or "*To Maggie and I.*" This oddity, which seems to have emerged only in the last twenty or so years, presumably arises from a feeling of discomfort about using the word *me*, a sense that it is somehow impolite or "uneducated." It may be that this has arisen from hearing other people saying "*Me* and Bill went out for beers." Whatever the reason, it is because this is such a major misapprehension, and such an egregious example of Bad English being used under the impression that it is somehow better than the English one would naturally speak and write, that we have used it as the title of this book.

See also ME, US, HIM/HER, THEM.

bored of We are *bored by* or *bored with* something or somebody. It is not at all good English to be *bored of* something or somebody (probably by analogy with "tired of"), although this usage has become increasingly common, especially among the young.

center "The tragedy of Oedipus *centers around* the fact that he has unknowingly killed his father and married his mother." Things have their *center* at a particular point and not *around* it; therefore Oedipus's tragedy should *center on* his unfortunate relationship with his parents.

change, sea, step Nowadays, it seems, it is impossible for a politician or a public spokesman of any kind to refer to a simple "change" or even to a "major change"; it must be a *sea change* or a *step change*.

A *sea change* is the kind of mysterious change wrought by long immersion in the sea which results in something quite unrecognizable, the reference of course being to Shakespeare's *The Tempest*: "But doth suffer a *sea change*, into something rich and strange."

A *step change* is a technical expression, referring to a change to an entirely different order, e.g., of number, such as from tens to thousands.

Most of the *changes* announced or promised by politicians are neither of the *sea* nor of the *step* variety.

chauvinism The word is derived from Nicolas Chauvin, a Napoleonic veteran noted, and in the end derided, for his extreme, unquestioning patriotism. The notion has long been extended into an unshakeable conviction of the superiority of any group or cause at the expense of other groups or causes; hence *economic chauvinism*, *white chauvinism,* and (since 1970) *male chauvinism*.

Most users of the last of these terms, perhaps coming on the word for the first time

James Cochrane

and ignorant of its earlier meaning, drop the *male* and refer simply to *chauvinism*. However, since there is still plenty of *chauvinism* of the old sort around, it might seem worthwhile to try to preserve the word in its original sense, adding *white* or *male* as appropriate.

cohort A *cohort* was a unit of the Roman army roughly equivalent to a battalion in modern armies. Later the word came to denote a number of persons united in a common cause or for a common purpose, or simply "supporters," "attendants," or whatever. For some time it has had a technical use in demographics as a group of persons having a statistical characteristic in common, particularly that of being born in the same year.

What it does not mean is "an associate" or "an accomplice," as in the sentence, "X was found guilty, along with his three *cohorts*." If the word is correctly used, a *cohort* cannot be a single person.

collateral damage A piece of euphemistic jargon that attempts to obscure through the use of "cool," abstract language the reality of death, maiming, and destruction of property among the civilian population as an unintended consequence of military action. For other euphemisms of this kind, see also FRIENDLY FIRE.

commence Except in formal contexts it is better to avoid this word and instead to use one of its humbler synonyms, *start* and *begin*.

community Rarely has a fine, even a noble, word been so devalued in recent times as this one has.

A *community* is a group of people living in close proximity and sharing their resources, to the extent even of eating at a common table. There were, and are, religious *communities* and "alternative" *communities* that live in this way. In a slightly looser sense there are town or neighborhood *communities* in which

James Cochrane

people know each other by name, go to each other's weddings and funerals, and share in communal activities such as town festivals and street parties; the television series *Ed* or *General Hospital* might be said to represent such *communities* in fictional form. Until quite recent times it was just about legitimate to write about "the Hollywood *community*," in that the stars, the producers, and the directors lived in close proximity, knew one another, met in the same restaurants and clubs, and were in a position to exchange fresh rather than warmed-up or recycled gossip.

But now we have the "gay *community*," the "Asian *community*," the "financial *community*," and even the "arts *community*"; phrases referring to large numbers of people widely dispersed geographically, mostly unknown to one another, and united only by such factors as sexual orientation, ethnicity, skill at making money out of money, or an interest in seeking subsidies from the taxpayer for cultural activities that would otherwise be unsustainable; in short, not *communities* in any real sense at all.

There are of course Asian, gay, and artistic *communities* in the true sense of the word, but that is a quite different matter. For general purposes it should be enough to say "most Asians," "most gays," etc.

Compare to/with Since the *com* part of *compare* means "with" it might be thought that it was always correct to say *"compare with"* and wrong to say *"compare to."* Those who believe this would have to answer to, among others, William Shakespeare, who wrote, "Shall I *compare* thee *to* a summer's day?" The rule of thumb is that *compare to* is correct when you are drawing attention to the similarities between two objects ("Shall I *say that you resemble* a summer's day?"). *Compare with* is to be preferred when we wish to note differences as well as or rather than similarities, as in *"Compared with* its mighty and quarrelsome neighbors, Ruritania is a quaint, untroubled, rather backward little country." Shakespeare, of course, goes on to say that no, he won't *compare* his mistress *to* a summer's day, and explains why not by conducting a detailed *comparison with* summer, in which the lady emerges as better in every respect—"more lovely and more temperate."

comprise, compose These two words bear a close relationship without being identical when correctly used. The basic rule is that the parts *compose* the whole; the whole *comprises* (or *consists of* or *is composed of*) the parts. Thus "A full deck *comprises* fifty-two cards," but "A good society is a means to a good life for those who *compose* it" (Bertrand Russell, quoted in the *Shorter Oxford English Dictionary*).

This distinction has been weakening for half a century or more, perhaps without much harm being done. But the typical real-estate agent's phrase "The property comprises of two living rooms and four bedrooms with baths" is seriously wrong and should be resisted; the same applies to the variant "*is comprised of.*" The correct alternatives would be "*comprises* two living rooms" or "*consists of…*" or "*is composed of….*"

consensus This is how the word should be spelled. It derives from Latin words meaning something like "the common feeling," hence "general agreement." The common spelling error *concensus* probably stems from confusion with *census* ("the official count of a population"), which has a quite different derivation.

contemporary Since at least the seventeenth century, *contemporary* has meant living or occurring at the same time, but there is a built-in ambiguity here: it can mean "living at the same time as each other," as in "Shakespeare was a contemporary of the composer John Dowland," or it can mean "living or occurring at the same time as us who are living now."

Because of its built-in ambiguity the word must be used with care. If a production of Shakespeare's *The Tempest* with *contemporary* music is announced, does this mean music by his *contemporary* John Dowland or by our *contemporary* composer Philip Glass? (We should be warned.)

coruscate In the print and broadcasting media, a review of a movie, book, or play is frequently described as *coruscating*. The user of this word presumably does not mean to suggest that the review is flattering, and is therefore on the face of it unaware that *to coruscate* means "to glitter, to throw off flashes of light."

Some of the reviews of Roger Ebert might correctly have been described as *coruscating*, but if the writer means to suggest that a review is designed to cause severe pain, the word he or she is almost certainly looking for is *excoriating,* from "to *excoriate,*" meaning "to flay, or to strip or rub the flesh off."

could of Educated readers will not need to be told that *could of* represents an illiterate mishearing of the contraction for *could have—could've*—and can never, in any circumstances, be correct English.

crescendo This is a musical term meaning a steady increase in volume of sound. (*Crescendo* is an Italian word meaning simply "increasing.") Since by definition a *crescendo* is a process that ends with maximum volume, it makes no sense to say that "the music was approaching its *crescendo*" or that "the violence reached a *crescendo*" as if the word meant "a peak" or "a climax."

criterion *Criterion* is a singular noun of Greek origin. Its plural is *criteria.* There are a great many supposedly educated people, including, for example, the "Education

James Cochrane

Correspondent" of the *Daily Telegraph* newspaper (November 21, 2001), who seem to be
unaware of this elementary fact.

See also PHENOMENON.

daily basis, on a See BASIS, ON A …

dangling participle "Walking up the familiar drive, the house seemed strangely quiet."

This is an example of a dangling, or unattached, participle. It offends against common sense as well as against the rules of grammar (which should after all have a basis in common sense), since obviously it is not the house that is walking up the drive but the person who is telling the tale. Writing "Walking up the familiar drive, I noticed that…" would have reattached the participle to its proper subject, "I," and saved the sentence from being nonsensical.

Here is another example, slightly more

complicated but equally wrong, from a Home Office advertisement in the *Times* (quoted in Burchfield, *The New Fowler's Modern English Usage*): "By giving this youngster the chance to repair and race old cars, he's not tempted to steal new ones." This might with advantage have read: "Our hope is that, by giving this youngster the chance to repair and race old cars, we'll help him to resist the temptation to steal new ones." In this latter version, the participial phrase "by giving this youngster the chance..." has been reattached to what it qualifies: "...we'll help him to resist...."

Examples of dangling or unattached participles abound in today's newspapers and broadcast media and even in books from respected publishers. Once recognized, they should be instantly zapped by the laser beam of common sense.

data The word *data* is a Latin plural of which the singular, *datum*, is nowadays very rarely used. In its modern meaning of "results in the form of facts and figures" it should, strictly speaking, be used with a plural verb, but in the world of computing it has become a singular noun, taking a singular verb.

decimate The word is obviously related to *decimal*, both being based on the Latin word for the number ten. The ancient Romans dealt with mutiny or cowardice in the army by selecting one man in ten, chosen by lot, for punishment, which normally meant death. *Decimated* is now often used instead of some such word as *devastated*, but should not be. When environmental activists claim that seals or other sea creatures are at risk of being *decimated* by an oil spill from a tanker, they presumably mean to suggest that many more than one in ten are likely to be killed or disabled. Statements such as "This small Palestinian township has been *decimated* in the recent conflicts" are equally unhelpful and misleading.

To *devastate*, by the way, means "to ruin utterly, to turn into a wasteland." In an age when such claims are often made it might be useful to have a word that means something more than *decimated* but less than *devastated*.

defuse, diffuse To *defuse* is literally to remove the fuse from an explosive device and figuratively to remove the tension from a potentially dangerous situation. To *diffuse* is to disperse. The two words should not be confused but frequently are, particularly in the "quality" newspapers.

déjà vu The French phrase, meaning literally "already seen," is correctly used to denote the feeling most of us have from time to time that we have seen or experienced something before, although in fact we are seeing or experiencing it for the first time. It is quite often wrongly used, especially by broadsheet journalists, to refer to something that has become boring or old hat because it has been seen or experienced once too often. If one wishes to use a French phrase for this, the correct one is *vieux jeu*.

deprecate, depreciate These two words have quite distinct meanings but are frequently confused.

To *deprecate* (from a Latin word meaning, literally, "to pray away" and hence "to ward off through prayer") is "to deplore, to heartily wish that something were elsewhere or otherwise than it is." In our time it has become familiar in a milder form as *self-deprecating*, which we can perhaps understand by imagining someone modestly waving away attention from him- or herself: "I pray you, pay no attention to little old *moi*!"

To *depreciate* likewise comes from a Latin word, in this case meaning "to lower the price." We can *depreciate* someone, in the sense of lowering or underestimating his or her worth, and our cars can, and mostly do, *depreciate* in the sense that they decrease in value.

derisive, derisory The two words are complementary, not synonymous, in correct modern usage. *Derisive* means "mocking"; *derisory* means "causing *derision*, ridiculous," as in "Management's latest offer is *derisory*. My members will greet it with *derisive* laughter."

deteriorate This is a Latinate word meaning simply "to get worse." If it is to be used at all it should be pronounced with all five syllables and not as *deteriate*.

diagnose "She was *diagnosed* with cancer."

This is an odd one. We dig with a spade, we eat with cutlery, we play golf with golf clubs. Yet for some reason we *diagnose* with a disease, rather than with *diagnostic* skills or instruments, as might have been expected. Perhaps the usage derives from such expressions as "He was down *with* flu" or "She was crippled *with* arthritis." Whatever the reason, this appears to be a Lost Cause, since the expression is nowadays used by medical "experts" as well as by ignorant laymen, but readers might still prefer to say, "*diagnosed* as having...."

didn't used   In John Lanchester's much-admired novel *The Debt to Pleasure* (1996) it is surprising to find his pedantic and supposedly erudite hero using the phrase "It *didn't used* to be" (along with a number of other historical and linguistic howlers, but no doubt the book is "postmodern" and "ironic"). This expression is extremely common, but if it were correct it would be the only occasion on which *didn't* is not followed by the infinitive form of the verb. We say "*didn't* walk," "*didn't* buy," "*didn't* go"; we don't say "*didn't* walked," "*didn't* bought," "*didn't* went." So why do we say "*didn't* used"?

It may be that the answer is that the verb "to use" in the sense of "to do as a customary practice" is never encountered in the present tense. We are "used to" saying that someone "used to" be or do something.

Therefore when we hear someone correctly say something like "He *didn't use* to wear gloves" (as Peter Cheney wrote in 1964) we have grown accustomed to hearing it as "*didn't used ....*" It is, nevertheless, an illiterate form of words that educated people should avoid, at least in writing.

different than That glorious book and national treasure, R. W. Burchfield's *The New Fowler's Modern English Usage* (Oxford University Press, Revised Third Edition, 1998) is surprisingly tolerant of *different than* (and of *different to*). In gently challenging those who would claim that it can never be "Good English," Burchfield uses powerful ammunition in the form of citations in the *Oxford English Dictionary* from as early as 1644, and he dismisses in his typically elegant yet kindly manner the argument that we say "x *differs from* y" and not "x *differs than* y" or "x *differs to* y," giving examples of other inconsistencies of that kind which are regarded as perfectly acceptable.

It is true that *than* normally follows a comparative, as in "bigger *than*," "faster *than*," etc. *Different* is not a comparative; its comparative form is "more *different*." No pedant could possibly quarrel with the sentence, "No two brothers could be more *different* in temperament *than* Cain and Abel," just as no pedant could accept the sentence, "Cain was *different than* Abel."

However, *than* also follows such noncomparatives as *rather* and *other*, and it is here that counsel for the defense of *different than* might find a chink through which a case for legitimacy might be made. It may well be that if *different than*, however mistaken, survives and prospers, it is because from time to time it avoids awkwardness of construction. Burchfield quotes an excellent example of this from *The Oxford Guide to English Usage* (1993): "Compare *The American Theatre, which is suffering from a different malaise than ours*, which is greatly preferable to *suffering from a* different malaise from that which ours is suffering from."

Nevertheless, Burchfield's conclusion is that "A wiser course, perhaps, is simply to avoid *different than.*" We are happy, and grateful, to be able to agree with him.

dilemma The expression "the horns of a *dilemma*" refers figuratively to a situation in which if a man manages to avoid one of the horns of an angry bull he is bound to be impaled on the other. This vividly illustrates the correct meaning of the word *dilemma*, which was once a term in logic but now denotes a situation in which one has to make a choice between two options, neither of which is particularly appealing.

Although etymologically there should be only two options, some authorities are nowadays willing to allow three or more, provided that they are known and can be stated. The important point, however, is that *dilemma* does not mean simply "a problem" or "an awkward decision to have to make."

discreet and discrete *Discreet* means "unobtrusive, circumspect, tactful." *Discrete* means "individually distinct, separate." Some writers, and even some publishers' editors, seem to be under the impression that *discrete* is a more up-market way of spelling *discreet*. If so, they are mistaken.

Note that the noun from *discreet* is *discretion*; the noun from *discrete* is *discreteness*.

disincentivise See INCENTIVISE.

disingenuous See INGENIOUS, INGENUOUS.

disinterested This is such an old favorite—in the 1980s it was the subject of more letters of complaint to the BBC than any other word, with the possible exception of *hopefully*—that one would expect everyone to know by now that *disinterested* ought to be used only in the sense of "impartial, having nothing personally to gain or lose," especially as the sense of "finding uninteresting, being bored by" is perfectly well served by *uninterested*. Nonetheless, what many old-fashioned people regard as a grave crime is still committed daily in speech and in print.

According to R. W. Burchfield in *The New Fowler's,* the matter is not quite as cut and dried as it appears, but it is surely a matter of practical common sense to preserve two separate words for two distinct meanings.

discuss We *discuss* something; we do not *discuss about* something.

disparate *Disparate* can mean either "markedly, essentially different" or—its older but nowadays rather less common sense—"unequal," as in "countries of *disparate* size." What it does not mean is merely *different*.

dissect To *dissect* is "to cut apart." The *dis-* is the same as the *dis-* in *dismember* and *dislocate* and many other words, and that is how the word should be pronounced. To pronounce it as *die-sect* is ignorant. The word *bisect* (to cut in two) is not a helpful analogy.

downsizing Euphemistic jargon for scaling down a commercial enterprise, almost invariably by means of cutting the numbers of staff employed in it.

See also LET GO, TO.

either … or If only for the sake of clarity *either* and *or* should be placed as closely as possible before the alternatives they refer to. For example, "He was determined to acquire *either* wealth *or* fame, and preferably both" is much better English than "He was *either* determined to acquire wealth *or* fame, and preferably both."

The same principle applies to *neither … nor*.

enervate To *enervate* is to deprive of nerve in the sense of spirit, energy, or courage; to be *enervated* is to be weakened or spiritless. Writers and speakers sometimes use the word *enervated* as if it were a synonym for *invigorated* or *energized*, but they could hardly be more mistaken.

envy and jealousy We are *jealous* of what is our own. We *envy* what belongs to others. Othello was driven to murder by strong sexual *jealousy* concerning his wife; in poisoning his mind against her, Iago was perhaps motivated by *envy* of Othello's glorious reputation as a successful general.

epicenter   *Epicenter* comes from Greek words meaning "upon a point" and is a technical term for the point on the earth's surface immediately above the point of origin of an earthquake. To use it as if it were an up-market substitute for the ordinary word *center*—as in "SoHo is the *epicenter* of Arts activity in the region"—is to invite ridicule.

equally as It is correct to say "The two men are *equally* stupid" or "One is *as* stupid *as* the other." It is quite wrong to conflate *equally* and *as* into "One is *equally as* stupid as the other."

equate We *equate* one thing *with* another; we do not *equate* one thing *to* another.

exclusive Things are *exclusive* by virtue of the fact that they *exclude*. An *exclusive* club excludes people not deemed suitable for election to membership. An *exclusive* hotel or resort excludes people who cannot afford its prices.

In the commercial world the word *exclusive* has come to mean either virtually nothing, as in a department store's advertising slogan "*Exclusively* for everyone," or some such notion as that "It looks much more expensive than it actually is."

If I receive in the post an "*exclusive* offer," why is it that so many of my neighbors have also received it?

executive An *executive* is someone who carries things out or gives effect to policy, nowadays often specifically a member of a relatively senior tier of management. So what is "*executive* housing," and what is an "*executive* car" or an "*executive* lounge"? Used in this way, *executive* seems to be a code word meaning "indicative of a certain level of salary and of a 'lifestyle' that is reassuringly middle class."

expatriate As a noun the word denotes someone living outside his or her own country and is so spelled and not as *expatriot*, which, if it existed as a word, would presumably mean "a former patriot."

fascination Broadly speaking, this means either "the action or faculty of compelling attention" or "the state of being *fascinated*." Snakes, supposedly, can *fascinate* their victims into a state of passivity by holding them with their eyes. However, care needs to be taken with this word. If we have a *fascination with* goldfish we quickly become absorbed in watching them and find it difficult to tear ourselves away. But if we have a *fascination for* goldfish they are irresistibly drawn to watching *us*. We should be clear about which of these two things we mean.

February This word has four syllables, the second of which begins with an *r*, but one would scarcely know this from the way it is pronounced by many speakers.

fine-toothed comb This is often sounded as if it were "*a fine toothcomb*" as in "They went through the documents with a *fine toothcomb*." So what exactly is a *toothcomb*? What is meant, of course, is a *fine-tooth* or *fine-toothed comb*, one capable, metaphorically, of thorough sifting or searching.

flout and flaunt "Saddam Hussein has continued to *flaunt* UN resolutions" (Tom Carver, BBC Washington Correspondent, September 2002).

At the time of writing, the only UN resolutions that Saddam Hussein would be likely to *flaunt* would be those that forbade any interference in Iraq's internal affairs. The BBC correspondent almost certainly meant to say *flout*.

To *flaunt* is "to display ostentatiously." To *flout* is "to break (rules or regulations) openly and even with contempt." The two words are very often confused, but should not be.

forensic This rather technical word means something like "pertaining to courts of law, legal argument, the procurement of evidence for a court of law, etc." *Forensic* medicine is medicine in the service of the court, but the word *forensic* by itself has nothing to do with medicine or with medical investigation.

fortuitous The word means "produced by chance, accidental," from the Latin word *forte*, "by chance." *Fortuitous* does not mean "fortunate" and *fortuitously* does not mean "by happy chance," but an increasing number of speakers and writers seem to be unaware of this.

fraught People who describe a situation as *fraught* seem to know what they mean to say, and people who hear them seem to understand what they are saying: that the situation is "distressing" perhaps, or "stressful," or just "tricky." They would probably be surprised to know that the original meaning of the word is "freighted" or "laden," so that a situation could at least in theory be *fraught* with delightful possibilities as well as with difficulties.

It is better to avoid the word unless we can say what something is *fraught* with, and it is never right to refer to "a *fraught* situation."

free gift Next time you are offered a *free gift*, ask yourself—or better still, the party offering it—whether there is any other kind, a *gift* being something that is given, not sold.

free rein To give *free rein* is to allow someone a considerable amount of freedom of action. The term comes from horse-riding and should be spelled *free rein* and not *free reign*, although the latter phrase, presumably meaning "unhindered rule," may have possibilities.

friendly fire Euphemism for fire originating from one's own side during military conflict as a result of misidentification, panic, or incompetence. The term was current during the war in Vietnam but became more widely known during the Gulf War of 1991 when, as in the Iraq conflict of 2003, several deaths and injuries were attributed to it. The expression strikes many as tasteless, but to date no one has come up with a more dignified alternative that has the same neatness.

See also COLLATERAL DAMAGE.

fulsome Since the seventeenth century the word has meant "excessively flattering, unctuous," as in the manner of Charles Dickens's Pecksniff toward those with whom he wishes to ingratiate himself. In the last half century, however, it has been increasingly used, mainly by politicians and journalists, as if it meant simply "full, generous," as in "a *fulsome* apology" or "a *fulsome* tribute." Burchfield also notes its use by fashion writers to mean "full-figured," perhaps by analogy with *handsome* or *wholesome*. The older meaning should be preserved, if only because it cannot so easily be replaced.

gerund, the This is certainly a Lost Cause, at least in the sense that very few people nowadays know what a *gerund* is. But just as people still use the *subjunctive* form without knowing the term itself—"He insisted that she *go* to bed immediately"—so the *gerund* survives in use, although largely unrecognized. The *gerund* is derived from a verb, usually by adding the suffix *–ing*. Although remaining a verb, it acts in some respects as if it were a noun, and especially in the respect that if the action denoted is attributed to someone or something it needs to be accompanied by the possessive form. A few examples should make this clearer: it is correct to say "We were surprised at *their* appearing so calm," "She was distressed at *his* leaving so suddenly," "I was surprised at *its* being so easy to do." It would be wrong to say "*them* appearing," "*him* leaving," or "*it* being."

graffiti Not many people, it seems, know that the word *graffiti* is the plural of the Italian *graffito*, meaning, originally, "a scratched inscription or drawing." *Graffiti* should therefore be used with a plural verb, but rarely is, even by supposedly educated speakers and writers.

Conversely, a single spray-painted slogan should be termed a *graffito*.

ground rules Correctly, the special *rules* pertaining to a particular playing-*ground*, course, or court—because, for example, of special physical features or size restrictions— and not, as widely supposed, the basic or fundamental *rules*.

guttural This should be so spelled, and not as *gutteral*. It is a term in phonetics denoting a sound produced in the throat and should not be used as if it meant simply "harsh, not mellifluous."

hare-brained This should be so spelled, the reference being to the apparently crazy behavior of *hares* in the rutting season. To spell it as *hairbrained* is an error.

hierarchy Note that this, and not *heirarchy*, is the correct spelling. It may help to know that the *hier-* part of the word derives from a Greek word meaning "sacred" or "priestly." The fact that *hier* sounds like "higher" is no doubt partly responsible for its having long ago strayed from its older meaning so as to include the notion of "ranking, order," as in "the corporate *hierarchy*."

hoi polloi These Greek words mean "the

many, the common people, the vulgar masses," *hoi* being the masculine plural of the definite article *the*. In English, it is an excusable mistake to say or write "the *hoi polloi*." However, it is not excusable to suppose, as some writers seem to do, that *hoi polloi* means "the rich, the plutocracy, the upper social set."

homogeneous The word, meaning "of the same kind," should be so spelled, with five syllables, and pronounced with the stress on the third syllable. It should not be confused, in spelling or pronunciation, with the scientific word *homogenous* (in biology or comparative anatomy, "having a common descent"), but often is.

homophobia This word seems to have been coined at some time during the 1970s to mean "fear or hatred of homosexuals, or of homosexuality." The persons responsible for coining it and putting it into circulation may or may not have been aware that the *homo-* part of the word *homosexual* derives from the Greek word *homos* meaning "the same," so that, strictly speaking, *homophobia* ought to mean "fear or hatred of things that are the same," perhaps the philosophy of those who believe that "variety is the spice of life."

However repugnant to lovers of the classical languages, *homophobia* must now be accounted a Lost Cause, if only because no one has been able to come up with an alternative, inoffensive word for a sentiment or attitude that seems to have been unknown to the ancient Athenians.

homosexual A British government minister recently announced that the word *homosexual* was to be banned from all government communications because it was "offensive." It is hard to see why, or to think of a more neutral, "value-free" way of denoting the condition of being "sexually drawn to one's own sex." It may be that there are still people who believe that the *homo-* part of the word comes from the Latin *homo* (which in any case means "human being" rather than "male"), whereas in fact it comes from the Greek *homos*, meaning "the same."

One can indicate an awareness of this by pronouncing the first syllable to rhyme with "Tom" rather than with "home."

hopefully Since the 1960s *hopefully* has been the favorite bugbear of language purists when used in such sentences as "*Hopefully* it will be over by Christmas." It is strange that this particular adverb should be singled out for hatred and ridicule in the way that it has, for its case is by no means unique.

Consider the following sentences: "*Frankly* I could do without it"; "*Sadly,* he died before I managed to reach him again"; "*Fortunately* I had enough money left to pay my fare home." It should be evident that these three adverbs do not directly qualify the verb in the sentence in which they appear. Instead they qualify the whole of the statement to which they are attached, indicating the spirit in which it is made. They are, in fact, sentence adverbs, and they could be said to be shorthand for longer expressions such as "To speak *frankly*" or "I am *sad* to say that..." or "It was *fortunate* that...." Robert Burchfield in *The New Fowler's Modern English Usage* explains that they have been used in this way since the seventeenth century but that the usage has become much more common since the 1960s. It may be that *hopefully*'s crime has been to be a relatively recent newcomer to the ranks of the sentence adverbs, but it is not at all clear that it deserves the condemnation it so often receives.

hyphen When verb phrases are used as nouns, it is usual and correct to insert a hyphen, as in *start-up*, *lay-offs*, *set-up*, *take-off*, *take-over*. It is sad to see how few editors realize that when these nouns revert to being verb phrases the hyphen is no longer needed and should go. It is ignorant to write "They intend to *start-up* a new company," "They are expected to *lay-off* some of the older workers," etc.

immanent, imminent The two words look and sound alike, but should not be confused.

Immanent means "inherent, pervading (creation or the universe)" and is most often found in religious or metaphysical contexts.

Imminent means simply "about to happen."

imply, infer In explaining the important difference between these two words it is probably impossible to improve on the example given by A. P. Herbert in *What a Word* (1935): "If you see a man staggering along the road you may *infer* that he is drunk, without saying a word, but if you say

'Had one too many?' you do not *infer* but *imply* that he is drunk."

In case any doubt remains, here is another example: "I *infer* from what you say that you do not believe my statement; you seem to *imply* that my word is not to be trusted."

In other words, *infer* means "deduce," and should not be used to mean *imply*, though it very often is.

incentivise Anyone with an ear for language will want to avoid this hideous recent coinage, meaning, presumably, "to give an incentive to," and its counterpart, *disincentivise*, meaning, presumably, "to withhold or withdraw an incentive." Both were used by "a government advisor on pension matters and governor of the London School of Economics" on the BBC's *Today* program on October 21, 2002.

in-depth To refer to an "*in-depth* analysis"

is not exactly Bad English, but never to use the word "analysis" without attaching *in-depth* to it is another example of autopilot English. The "analysis" could also be *thorough* or *exhaustive*, or for that matter *sloppy* or *superficial*.

industry Not long ago, one sense of the word *industry* was in reference to the activity of manufacturing concerns, whether *heavy*, as in coal mining, steelmaking, shipbuilding, etc., or *light*, as in pharmaceuticals, textiles, etc.; in short, the kind of manufacturing activity that involved numbers of "manual" workers.

At some time in the 1960s, many people of the kind Marxists used to call "workers by brain" seem to have decided to claim their share of the nobility of labor by designating their activities as "*industrial*." Thus we now have "the financial services *industry*," "the publishing *industry*," "the classical music *industry*," "the Sylvia Plath *industry*," and so forth.

ingenious, ingenuous These are two very similar words with quite distinct meanings that should not be confused.

The current meaning of *ingenious* is "clever or skillful in a sense suggestive of complexity or intricacy," as in "an *ingenious* device" or "a most *ingenious* criminal."

Ingenuous means "frank, open, artless, even naïve."

To be *disingenuous* is in effect to be a great deal less *ingenuous* than one is pretending to be.

The noun from *ingenious* is, oddly enough, *ingenuity*; the noun from *ingenuous* is *ingenuousness*.

in terms of Properly used, this prepositional phrase declares the terms in which a statement is claimed to be true: "*In terms of* numbers of men, tanks, and other *matériel*, the French in the spring of 1940 were superior to the German forces opposing them; *in terms of* other factors, such as *morale* and communications, they were, as it soon turned out, sadly inferior."

In terms of is still occasionally used correctly in this way, but in recent times it has started to behave like an irresistible virus, destroying and replacing such old familiar words and phrases as *concerning* or *as regards* or *in view of* or *in the light of* or even simply *about*, to the extent that one now seems to hear or read it a hundred times a day.

One very recent example demands to be quoted: discussing a cricketer's decision not to play for the English touring team after all, a speaker on BBC radio declared that "his attitude is not surprising *in terms of* the personal crisis he has been going through." Not long ago he would surely have said "*in view of....*"

Perhaps this is not yet a Lost Cause. Perhaps *in terms of* is one of those modish phrases that sooner or later become wearisome through repetition. Perhaps before not too long it will be thought off to ask

"What's your opinion *in terms of* Gordon Brown?" Let us hope so.

irregardless This clownish word is so well disguised as a sensible one that it quite often slips by unnoticed, used in place of *regardless*—as in "*irregardless* of the consequences"—whereas what it means literally is "*not regardless*." It is presumably a conflation of *regardless* and *irrespective* and is sometimes used in jest, sometimes in ignorance.

In a similar vein, a spokesman for local government chief executives recently stated that the government was "paying scant *disregard*" to some problem or other.

is repeated "The question *is*, *is* whether..."; "The point *is*, *is* that..."; "The fact of the matter *is*, *is* that..."; even "The difficulty *is*, *was* that...."

This mysterious, and quite meaningless, repetition of the word *is* (or *was*) was first noted by an American scholar in the 1971 but may now be heard on the BBC countless times in the course of a normal day. It has even been recorded on the lips of notable politicians representing all the major British political parties! Examples of it have been printed above with a comma after the first *is* to indicate a brief pause, but it is frequently heard without any pause at all between the *is*es.

It is frequently heard, but it is rarely, if ever, seen in print, perhaps because to see it written is at once to recognize its absurdity. So the question is, why do people repeat the word *is* (or *was* for that matter)? Could it be that in putting strong emphasis on the initial phrase—"*the point is!*"—they hear it in their heads as "the *important* point, the point that I am trying to stress" and in doing so fail to notice that first *is*? If so, this is an explanation, but it is not an excuse. This is English that is not only bad, but stupid, and it should be mocked and jeered at until it disappears out of sheer embarrassment.

issue The recent history of this word has been fascinating. A century or so ago it meant, as an intransitive verb, "to come forth," as in "the words that *issued* from his lips." As a noun it meant "that which comes forth," as in "the *issue* of his loins," or it meant "the outcome, the result," as in "the *issue* was in doubt." In a legal context it meant "the point in question" and, by extension, "a matter that is in contention or that remains to be decided." By the late nineteenth century it had come also to mean "an item given out or supplied," as in "army *issue*."

In the course of the Second World War, language purists became greatly exercised when that last usage led to what was regarded as the hideous verb formation *to issue with*, as in "the men were *issued with* clean underwear," which certainly represented a real departure in meaning from the intransitive to the transitive. Rightly or wrongly, that meaning of the verb *to issue* is now firmly established.

What has happened more recently is that, in some circles at least, what was at one time the legal usage of the noun *issue*—"question, matter to be decided"—has virtually replaced all the others. As used by such interest groups as the feminists, it has now more or less displaced the words *question* and *problem*, so that we have such statements as "I don't have any *issues* with that" or "Soap opera plot lines are mainly *issue*-based" or "she has *issues* about gender differentiation."

This is not, strictly speaking, Bad English, but it is becoming wearisome, and we must hope that it is a fashion that will one day pass.

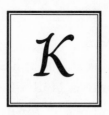

key The word *key* has long been used figuratively to suggest "that which unlocks a mystery or removes an obstruction" or—no doubt from the idea of a *keystone*—"central, indispensable, pivotal." Recently, however, its use as an adjective has gone to absurd lengths to give us such expressions as "this is absolutely *key*," which thoughtful people will certainly want to avoid.

kind of *Kind* is a noun, its plural is *kinds*; therefore the normal rules about singular and plural ought to apply to it. Yet phrases such as "those *kind of* people" are almost more common nowadays than the correct and logical usage, which would of course be "that *kind of* person."

It is almost as if *kind of* has been silently hyphenated into a kind of adjective, but there is no good reason for it, and educated speakers should stick to the logical practice.

Kind of is also used colloquially as an adverb in ways that suggest that the speaker is giving only an approximate sense of what he or she wants to say, as in "I felt *kind of* sad" or "I *kind of* thought you wouldn't come" or "It was *kind of* beige." This is now an acceptable part of informal speech but should of course be avoided in more formal contexts.

L

latter "He had four sons, the *latter* of whom died in infancy." *Latter* in this sentence should be *last*. *The latter* should be used only of the second item of a pair, corresponding to *the former*.

lead The past tense of the verb *to lead* is *led*, not *lead*. There is nothing logical about this—the past tense of *read* is *read*, not *red*—but it is how it is.

leading question In a court of law, an alert judge will be quick to restrain counsel from asking a *leading question* of a witness. A *leading question* is one that suggests to the witness the answer that counsel is looking for: "Did you then see the accused pull out a revolver and shoot Officer Bucket?" would be an example. The permissible question would be: "What did you see then?"

Among laypeople the phrase is used as if it meant an important or an intrusive question or one that required the person questioned to say more than he or she cared to, but none of these is its correct meaning.

less and fewer *Less* describes quantity; *fewer* describes number. For example: "For a healthy diet we should eat *less* sugar, salt, and animal fat and *fewer* sweets and chocolates," or "in order to weigh *less* we should consume *fewer* calories." It is Bad English to write e.g., "There were *less* accidents on the roads last year than in any year since 1958."

The normal rule is that *fewer* is used with nouns that have plurals and *less* is used with nouns that have no plural in ordinary discourse, such as "sand," "chatter," "food," "trouble," "praise," or "oil."

When we are describing a number itself, *less* is correct. Thus: "*Fewer* than fifty people were injured" but "The eventual death-toll was *less* than twenty."

See also AMOUNT, NUMBER.

let go, to This is one of several current euphemisms for dismissing someone from employment. What is offensive about it is the genteel pretense that one is allowing an employee to leave rather than firing him or her.

The word *euphemism* derives from a Greek word meaning "use of an auspicious word for an inauspicious one." To quote R. W. Burchfield: "The use of euphemisms can be traced back to the Middle Ages, but the prevalence of such evasive and concealing (or fair-sounding) terminology has never been more marked than in the cruel social and political areas of life in the 20c" (*The New Fowler's Modern English Usage*).

See also COLLATERAL DAMAGE.

liaise, liaison These are sometimes found spelled *liase* and *liason* but should not be. They are incorrectly used if they lose the sense of a link or connection between two things or two parties.

lie and lay *To lay* is a transitive verb, i.e., one that takes an object, as in "To *lay* a brick"; to *lie* is an intransitive verb, i.e., one that does not take an object, as in "We *lie* down." The past tense of *lay* is *laid* ("We *laid* a brick") and so is the passive voice ("The brick was *laid*"); the past tense of *lie* is *lay* ("We *lay* down") and the perfect tense is *have lain*; being an intransitive verb it cannot have a passive form.

Expressions such as "He was just *laying* there, dead drunk" are recognized regional usages, but are not standard English.

light year If this expression is to be used it is important to recognize that it is a unit of distance—the distance that light travels in one year, or around 6 million million miles—and not of time.

like and as See AS AND LIKE.

literally "The Iranians are *literally* glued to their television screens" (correspondent on the BBC World Service during the war in Iraq, April 2003).

Literally means...*literally*. It means that we mean, to the letter, exactly what we are saying, or in other words that we are not speaking figuratively. If, therefore, we say, "I was *literally* climbing the walls with anxiety" or "He was *literally* drowning in debt" or "They were *literally* glued to their television screens," then we are using the word in *literally* the opposite of its correct sense and committing a serious abuse of our language.

loathe and loath The verb *to loathe*, meaning "to detest," as in "I *loathe* broccoli," is so spelled, with the *th* sound pronounced hard, as in *breathe*. The adjective, meaning "reluctant," as in "I was *loath* to depart," is correctly spelled as either *loath* or *loth*, with the *th* pronounced softly, as in *breath*.

lowest common denominator "The BBC seems to be trying to appeal to the lowest common denominator of public taste." That may well be true, but the fact is that in mathematics the lowest common denominator is a relatively high number—the lowest common denominator of 2, 3, 4, and 6 is 12—whereas the highest common factor is a relatively low number—the highest common factor of 12 and 18 is 6. But since this is no longer widely understood, and since the speaker or writer is trying to convey the idea of lowness rather than highness, this must be accounted a Lost Cause.

majority The word *majority* should be used of numbers or of countable nouns, i.e., nouns that have plurals (e.g., "the *majority* of Americans"). It should emphatically not be used of uncountable nouns, as in e.g., "he inherited the *majority* of the estate." In that last case one should say and write "the *major* part" or "the *greater* part" or, quite simply, "*most*."

may and might "Even so, without the Depression and the calamitous effect upon Germany from the end of that year, the Nazi Party *may* well have broken up and faded into oblivion" (Ian Kershaw, *Hitler 1889–1936*, italics added).

"A mentally ill man *may* not have committed suicide had he been kept in hospital, rather than been discharged to be cared for in the community" (*Guardian*, 1990, italics added).

A tour guide addressing a group near Slough, Bucks: "And there is Eton College, where Prince Charles *may* have gone to school" (italics added).

In all of these examples *may* should be *might*. This is not simply a matter of grammatical pedantry but of clarity and common sense. What the tour guide appears to say is that it is possible that, unknown to the British public, the Prince of Wales attended the famous public school convenient for one of the family homes in Windsor rather than, as we had thought, his father's alma mater, Gordonstoun. What he presumably *means* to say is that there *was* a possibility at one time that Charles would go to Eton.

In precisely the same way, Professor Kershaw, if taken literally, appears to suggest that it is possible that the Nazi party disappeared in 1929 and the *Guardian* that it is possible that the unfortunate man did not, after all, commit suicide. In all three cases, any ambiguity would have been removed simply by the use of *might* rather than *may*. The general rule is that *may* represents a possibility that still exists, while *might* represents a possibility that existed at some time in the past but did not materialize at that time.

It should be a matter of grave concern that the word *might* as the past tense of *may* seems to be in danger of disappearing from both written and spoken English. The cost, in terms of simple clarity of meaning, is considerable, as the above examples illustrate. The problem is exacerbated when "quality" newspapers and leading academics (and their publishers' editors) make this elementary error and thereby set such a poor example to those who don't feel completely confident in their use of the language.

Is this a case like that of *between you and I*? Does the writer fear for some reason that the use of the word *might* is somehow incorrect or impolite? If so, readers, take courage! *Might* is (quite often) right.

me, us, him/her, them   "Gloaters jab fingers at *we* who opposed the war, saying we have been proved wrong" (Polly Toynbee, *Guardian*, April 16, 2003, italics added).

"They sent my brother and *I* to boarding school" (Rory Bremner on "Desert Island Discs," April 2003).

"The sexual tension *between he* and Norris as Di Jordan seems bizarrely disconcerting" (From a television review in the *Daily Telegraph* listings supplement).

A strange disease is afflicting supposedly educated writers and speakers of English, and the last of the three quotations above (which might be the first recorded case of a new variant) suggests that it is becoming even more virulent. It takes the form of extreme nervousness amounting almost to terror concerning the use of *me, us, him/her,* and *them,* the accusative forms of the personal pronouns *I, we, he/she,* and *they.* Did Polly Toynbee (or, just possibly, her editor at the *Guardian*) feel that to say "jab fingers at *us*" would be somehow uncouth? Did the excellent Rory Bremner think that it would be ill-mannered to talk of "my brother and *me*"? Without further investigation it is impossible to say. As for the reviewer in the *Daily Telegraph* listings supplement, if a quick cure cannot be found it is to be hoped he has been quarantined to prevent further spreading of the disease.

See also BETWEEN YOU AND I.

media It should go without saying, but does not, that *media* is the plural of *medium.* The word is most usually found nowadays as shorthand for "the *media* of communication," that is, the print and broadcast *media,* often personified so as to include the people who own and work in these *media*. *Media* is nonetheless a plural noun and should be used with a plural verb, as in "the *media* have less influence on voters than their owners would like to believe." Statements such as "The media was present in large numbers" should be avoided.

militate and mitigate   These two words have quite distinct meanings that should not be, but often are, confused.

To *militate* (usually followed by "against") is "to have weight, force, or effect," as in, "Brilliant though he was, the notorious irregularities of his private life *militated* against his reaching the higher offices of government."

To *mitigate* is "to make less severe, to moderate," as in the "*mitigating* circumstances" that might persuade a judge to reduce the sentence on a convicted felon.

minuscule   This word, which nowadays

means simply "very small," used to have a very particular meaning, referring to small manuscript letters as distinct from capitals. The important point is that it should be spelled *minuscule* and not, as so often, *miniscule*.

mission statements No public body these days, it seems, feels it has done its duty until it has produced what it will probably call a "mission statement" in the form of a participial phrase: "Providing jobs and services" (typical town council), "Working to make London safer" (the Metropolitan Police), and so forth. Two noticed recently are: "Making knowledge work" (the University of Bradford) and "Connecting people with God" (St. Mary's Church of England, Islington, London).

What is it about these phrases that is so irritating? In the case of St. Mary's, Islington, perhaps it is the sheer *vulgarity* of reducing the *raison d'être* of the church to a glib commercial slogan, no doubt in the name of "accessibility," "relevance," or "youth appeal." More generally it may be a sense of the essential dishonesty of "statements" which, like the verbless sentences of Prime Minister Tony Blair, are not really statements at all but merely vague aspirations for which no one can properly be held to account.

It might be an amusing game to invent more truthful versions of some of these statements; in the case of the first two mentioned above perhaps "Spending lots of your money on creating jobs for our political supporters" and "Trying to make London safer by charging around its streets in fast cars."

moment in time, at this This is an example of what might be called "speaking on autopilot." The phrase *this moment* automatically triggers the follow-up, *in time*. But if a *moment* is not "*in time*" then what is it in? For Einstein and his successors it might be important to make a distinction, but for ordinary mortals it is surely enough to say *at this moment* or even, simply, *now*.

myriad This was originally a Greek word meaning "ten thousand." It long ago came to mean "a very large number, uncountable," as in "a *myriad* of butterflies" and must be accounted a Lost Cause.

neither...nor See EITHER...OR.

no sooner...when/barely...than It is surprising how often one reads sentences such as "*No sooner* had I got into the house *when* the telephone rang" or "*Barely* had she entered the room *than* she was spotted by her ex-husband."

Simple common sense rather than any notion of grammatical correctness would surely suggest that the comparative *sooner* should be followed by *than* and that the simple adverb *barely* (or *scarcely* or *hardly*) should not be.

not enough ands "The scandal was headline

news, seriously damaging the credibility of the president, the Republican Party, and giving a considerable boost to the lagging Democrats."

"Southern Scotland, North and East England will remain dry" (typical BBC weather forecast).

Many readers would sense that there was something wrong with these sentences without being able to say immediately what the something was; it is in fact the absence of an *and* between "the president" and "the Republican Party" in the first sentence and between "Scotland" and "North" in the second. Once that *and* is inserted and the comma removed, the meaning of the sentence is clarified (and the rhythm greatly improved).

What has happened in sentences of this kind is that the writer, or perhaps the writer's editor, has somewhat mindlessly applied an editorial "rule" that states that in a list of more than two items or elements all *ands* should be removed except the final one. This is a rather crude rule that the best writers of English have felt free to ignore when it suits them—imagine Wordsworth writing:

"Roll'd round in Earth's diurnal course,
With rocks, stones, and trees."

But in any case the rule has been misapplied in the examples given above. In the first sentence there are in fact two verbs after "headline news"—"damaging" and "giving"—and the first verb is followed by only two items—"the president" and "the Republican Party"—which therefore demand to be linked by *and* rather than by a comma. In the weather forecast, "North" is not a noun, but one of two adjectives qualifying "England."

As with so many examples of Bad English in this book, errors of this kind have begun to crop up regularly only in the last twenty or thirty years, reflecting once again the triumph of half-educated over both educated and uneducated speech.

not only...but also As in the case of EITHER...OR, it is important to place *not only* where it logically belongs, which generally means not dropping it in too early. For example, "He *not only* wrote history *but also* light fiction" is wrong; the sentence should read "He wrote *not only* history *but also* light fiction."

"He *not only* wrote history *but also* gave piano lessons" is also correct.

not so much This is perfectly good English provided that it is followed by *as* and not by *but*. "*Not so much* a job *as* a way of life" is good English; "*Not so much* a job *but* a way of life" is not.

nouns as verbs A rather unwelcome development is the practice of using nouns as verbs. *To impact, to source* (or *outsource*), *to track,* and *to fast-track* are examples now encountered every day, and there will no doubt be many more by the time this book is in print. They are part of a dreadful new and actually rather sinister bureauspeak that deserves a book to itself because the way it displaces thought and subverts meaning needs more discussion than there is room for here. George Orwell encountered an earlier version of it, which he analyzed in his classic essay "Politics and the English Language."

nuclear This is the adjective from *nucleus* and should be pronounced *new-clee-ar* or possibly *nooclee-ar* but not *noo-cue-lar*.

off of To say and write *off of*, as in "It fell *off of* a truck," is not acceptable in standard English. "It fell *off* a truck" is correct English irrespective of the truth or falsehood of the statement.

on a daily basis See BASIS, ON A ...

ongoing situation Another example of autopilot-speak. If a *situation* is not *ongoing* has it not ceased to be a *situation* at all?

only The rule that *only* should be placed only before the word it is intended to qualify is one that is often broken even by the best writers, but there are occasions when failure to place it carefully can cause confusion.

The extent to which its placing can alter meaning was delightfully illustrated by Marghanita Laski in the *Observer* in April 1963 (quoted by Burchfield in *The New Fowler's*). She describes how at her preparatory school pupils were asked to place *only* in every possible position in the sentence, "The peacocks are seen on the western hills": "*Only* the peacocks..."; "The *only* peacocks..."; "The peacocks are *only*..."; etc.

oral, verbal The two words should not be confused. *Oral* means literally "of or with the mouth," hence, of a statement, "spoken." *Verbal* means "in words." A *verbal* statement, agreement, or whatever may be spoken or written. A *nonverbal* communication is one that manages without words.

outplacement This is another euphemism

for the dismissal of one or more employees in a bid to save costs.

See also LET GO, TO.

panacea This derives from a Greek word meaning "all-healing" or "cure-all"; hence "a universal remedy," whether literally, in a strictly medical sense, or metaphorically, in a wider sense. However the word is used, it is terrible to say or write "a *panacea* for all ills" or "a universal *panacea*," since the idea of universality is already implicit in the word itself. For the same reason, it is an error to attach the word to a particular ailment, as in "a *panacea* for the common cold."

paradigm shift "The Job: To work with patients, professional groups, and other to achieve a *paradigm shift* in patients' experiences of healthcare in England." (Help wanted advertisement in the *Guardian*'s Society pages, April 7, 2004. Italics added.)

What exactly is a *paradigm shift*? The term has a technical meaning in the philosophy of science, but here it seems to mean nothing more than "a complete change" (presumably for the better). See also CHANGE, SEA, STEP

peninsula(r) The noun is *peninsula*. *Peninsular* is the adjective, but is depressingly often used as if it were the noun.

perspicacious, perspicuous These two words should either be used with great care or else avoided in favor of rather simpler synonyms such as *perceptive* and *lucid*, not least because some of the greatest writers have sometimes confused them and their derivatives.

To oversimplify somewhat, *perspicacious* can be used only of a person and means "clear-sighted, discerning, shrewd." The noun derived from it may be *perspicacity* or *perspicaciousness*.

Perspicuous is normally applied only to things and means, literally, "easy to see through"; hence "clear, lucid, easily understood." The corresponding noun is either *perspicuity* or *perspicuousness*.

phenomenon This is a noun of Greek origin; its plural form is *phenomena*, but, as with CRITERION, this simple fact seems to be beyond the mental competence of many politicians and "media people."

prefer...than "I *prefer* to get wet *than* carry an umbrella" is Bad English. Correct usages are "I would *rather* get wet *than* carry an umbrella" or "I *prefer* to get wet *rather than* carry an umbrella" or "I *prefer* getting wet *to* carrying an umbrella."

prestige At one time this word answered to its Latin derivation and conveyed the sense of "illusion or delusion," with special reference to the deceptive tricks of a juggler or what would nowadays be called a "magician" or a "conjuror." By the nineteenth century it had acquired its present meaning of "reputation," either "glamorous" or, more recently, "both glamorous and of thoroughly sound value," as in "A prestige address" or a "prestige car."

The same history applies to the adjective *prestigious*. The change in meaning is great, but is perhaps not greatly to be regretted, since we have no word for *prestige*...except *prestige*.

prevaricate, procrastinate The two words are quite distinct in meaning.

To *prevaricate* is to do what politicians are particularly skilled at: avoiding a direct answer to a question, quibbling, acting evasively.

To *procrastinate* is to delay, to put off endlessly, *cras* being the Latin word for tomorrow.

principle, principal These two words should not be confused, but often are.

Principle is only ever used as a noun, meaning "a fundamental truth or law as the basis of reasoning or action," as in "He always stuck by his *principles*."

Principal is either an adjective meaning "most important, chief" or a noun referring to the chief person, e.g., the head administrator of a school, or a leading character in a film or a play, or, in a special sense, a capital sum as distinct from the interest earned from it.

prior to This means nothing more or less than *before* and it is hard to think of circumstances in which it would not be better to say and write *before* rather than *prior to*.

privilege Not long ago in Britain, the National Association of Teachers of English urged an education minister not to *privilege* standard English over regional and working-class dialects, meaning presumably that standard English should not be granted greater importance than nonstandard English. Apart from the questionable wisdom of this advice, which would in effect limit the command of a universally comprehensible version of the language to a *privileged* minority, it is depressing to see *privilege* used as a verb in this way. Fortunately, however, the usage seems to be confined to the more fashionable and foolish elements of the academic "community."

See also NOUNS AS VERBS

procrastinate See PREVARICATE.

prophecy, prophesy The noun is spelled *prophecy*; the verb is spelled *prophesy*.

protagonist In ancient Greek drama the was the principal actor. The *pro*-part of the word is from the Greek word *protos*, "first," and there was originally only one *protagonist*.

Over the centuries it has become acceptable to use *protagonists* in the plural to mean the chief persons in a drama or in a situation. It is still wrong, however, to put the word *leading* or *main* or *chief* in front of it, since that is implicit in the first syllable, *pro-*.

What is even more wrong is to use the word to mean "a supporter, a proponent, an advocate," as in "She was an early *protagonist* of women's rights," on the mistaken assumption that the *pro-* is the Latin prefix meaning "for, in favor of," and that therefore *protagonist* is the opposite of *antagonist*.

quantum leap Not only is this now a rather tiresome cliché but its journalistic use as meaning "a sudden and dramatic increase in scale or quantity" has always been mistaken. *Quantum leap*, or *quantum jump*, is a term from the world of subatomic particles, in which it means something like "an abrupt transition from one *quantum* state to another," and should be left to people who are at home with such matters.

reason…because It is better to avoid the construction *The reason is because…* because it is rather like saying *The reason is for the reason that…*. It is normally sufficient to say *The reason is that…*.

reason being, the A speaker on a BBC natural history broadcast states that "Numbers of this particular species have declined to worryingly low levels in recent years, and *the reason being is* that its habitat is being eroded by modern farming practices." He might have said "…have declined…in recent years, and the reason *is*…" or "…have declined…in recent years, *the reason being* that…." Instead, for some reason he decided to wear both belt and suspenders and produced "*the reason being is.*"

Why do people make this kind of mistake? It should go without saying that educated speakers don't say "*the reason being is,*" but one suspects that thirty years ago uneducated speakers would not have done so either. As with so many other cases in this book, might it be that modern educational methods have produced more rather than less insecurity about the way we use our language? Is it anxiety about some mistaken notion of "correctness" that leads us into such absurdities as this one?

recrudescence   This word is quite often used as if it meant simply "a return, a revival." It is in fact a medical word meaning "the breaking out again of a disease, the renewed inflammation of a wound," etc.; its Latin origin lies in words meaning "making raw again." In other words, *recrudescence* is rarely good news except for those hoping to benefit from the decease of a rich relative.

referendum This was once a Latin gerundive meaning "requiring to be referred"; its Latin plural is *referenda*. In modern English the only use of the word *referendum* is for the practice of referring a question to the vote of the entire electorate. Since the practice invariably involves only one question—for example, whether the United Kingdom should join the Single European Currency or whether Swiss women should be given the vote—the correct plural in English is *referendums*, not *referenda*. *Referenda* would mean "matters requiring to be referred."

See also AGENDA.

refute To *refute* is to disprove by argument or by the production of evidence. It is not simply to *deny*, and police officers, football players, and politicians who state that they "*refute*" allegations made against them are usually merely *denying* them.

resources This is a perfectly good word that is, however, used with increasing frequency as a euphemism for "money" or "funding," especially by people who, for one reason or another, find it embarrassing to admit that what they are demanding is simply more cash, as in "Our members simply cannot meet their health and safety responsibilities to the public without more *resources*."

It is often found in contexts in which excuses are being sought for some failure of courage, efficiency, or common sense, as in "The local authority's failure to protect the children in its care from serious abuse is entirely down to lack of *resources*."

The game is given away completely when the word is used as a singular noun, *resource* (i.e., "money")—as in "what is needed is more *resource*"—or as a verb, *to resource* (i.e., "to fund"). Next time you hear some official spokesman talking about *resources*, ask yourself—or, if you can, ask him or her—exactly what he or she means by it.

restaurateur The owner of a restaurant is a *restaurateur*, literally "a restorer." Traditionally he promises to "restore" our spirits and our physical well-being with his excellent food and wine. Neither in English nor in French does the word *restauranteur* properly exist.

restructuring This is often nowadays used as a euphemism for the process by which costs are reduced in a commercial organization by shedding staff, e.g., after a takeover or a merger.

See also DOWNSIZING.

reticent Not long ago, the education correspondent of the *Times* of London stated that teachers were "reticent to talk about violence in the classroom." Since *reticent* means "disinclined to speak freely; reserved," this could fairly be described as a tautology. *Reticent* does not mean simply "reluctant," a word that would have served the education correspondent perfectly well in making her statement. This is one example out of many in which half-educated people use the wrong word in the belief that it is somehow smarter or more sophisticated than the plain old right one.

rites of passage Rituals attending the passage from one stage of life to another, especially from youth to adulthood. *Right of passage* means something else entirely, e.g., the right of Russian naval vessels to pass through the Dardanelles Strait into the Mediterranean.

S

sacrilegious This should be so spelled, and not as *sacreligious*. The latter misspelling probably results from the mistaken belief that the word has some etymological connection with *religion*. It does not.

safe haven A *haven* is by definition a *safe* place for a ship to shelter in. An *unsafe haven* would be a contradiction in terms.

secretary There is a normal, educated pronunciation of this word, with an *r* at the beginning of the second syllable, and there is a special pronunciation favored by trade union officials, politicians, and others, namely *secketary*.

show, showed, shown The past tense of *show* is *showed* ("The agent *showed* me the house"). The past participle may be *shown* ("He has *shown* it to me") or *showed*, but *shown* is preferable. The passive form should always be *shown* ("It has been *shown*").

singular and plural "For many people perceptions of greater community spirit is a positive advantage for residents" (*State of the Countryside 2002:* Report from the Countryside Agency).

It is quite remarkable these days how often, in speech and in print, we find cases such as the above, in which the number (singular or plural) of the verb is taken, not from the subject of the verb (in this case, "perceptions"), but from the nearest noun (in this case, "spirit").

What can be the reason for what is not merely ungrammatical English but actually *stupid* English? Is it that the writer or the speaker has such a short attention span that halfway through the sentence he or she has forgotten how it started out? If so, the young woman who recently said on the BBC *Today* program, "The diversity of these books *are* terrific," must have a very short attention span indeed, as must also the "education spokesman" who, even more recently, referring to the theft of examination papers, declared, "The security of the papers *are* questionable."

And why is it that these strange lapses almost never occurred before c. 1990? Might it have something to do with the coming of age of a generation that went to primary school in the educationally "progressive" late 1960s?

slither, sliver A *sliver* is a slice, usually a very thin one, for example of *prosciutto*. The word is surprisingly often confused with *slither,* a verb meaning "to move in a slippery fashion."

sort of See KIND OF.

stationary, stationery The adjective meaning "not moving" is spelled *stationary*. The noun meaning, broadly, "writing materials" is spelled *stationery*.

still continues Is any meaning lost if one says, simply, *continues*?

straitjacket, strait-laced The *strait-* in these words means "narrow, tight." A *straitjacket* is designed to confine the arms of someone who might otherwise do damage to himself or others. Someone who is *strait-laced* is, in figurative terms, "tightly corseted," hence "prudish, puritanical." Spellings with *straight-* are not acceptable.

stratum The correct plural form is *strata*, which should be followed by a plural verb.

suffice to say If one is going to use this

rather old-fashioned expression, one should get it right: *suffice it to say*, meaning "let it be enough to say." *Suffice to say* is ignorant and lazy.

supersede This is the correct spelling. There is no such word as *supercede*.

syndrome This is a word of Greek origin, meaning literally "running together." In its original medical sense it refers to a condition in which two or more symptoms appear together without any obvious causal link between them, as in Severe Acute Respiratory Syndrome, of which breathing difficulties are only one of the symptoms. It may be quite properly used by extension into a wide range of characteristic combinations of behavior, opinions, etc., but it is important to retain the sense of two or more elements running together, rather than a single one.

$\mathcal{T}$

talisman The word derives from an Arabic via a Greek word, and the *-man* part of it has nothing to do with the species *Homo sapiens*. The plural is therefore *talismans*, not *talismen*.

tandem, in People, animals, or things *in tandem* are one in front of the other rather than side by side. (The expression has a rather jokey derivation from the Latin word *tandem* meaning "at length.") Thus horses may be harnessed *in tandem* or a couple may jointly pedal a *tandem* bicycle. The phrase does not mean simply "jointly" or "together."

target When using this word in a sense other than its literal one it is important to remember that a *target* may be aimed at, hit, missed, set at a greater or lesser distance, or removed, but not pursued, achieved, attained, kept to, obtained, increased, or kept abreast of.

As a verb, meaning something like "to designate as a *target*," it should be used with care, if at all.

task force This is originally a military term for an *ad hoc* group of different types of unit brought together for a specific mission. Metaphorical use in nonmilitary contexts may occasionally be justified, but a *task force* is not simply a "working party" or a "sub-committee" or any other body likely to produce minutes rather than results.

tenterhooks, on The phrase, meaning "impatient, as if with nerves tautly strung," is so spelled and not as *on tenderhooks*.

throes of, in the This is how the expression should be spelled. When seen in the form "*in the throws of*" it should be treated with ridicule and contempt.

transpire This word once had (and still has) a technical meaning in the contexts of botany, biology, and physics. Its present-day, nontechnical, figurative meaning—"to come to light, to emerge, to leak out, to become clear"—would at one time have been deplored, but is now entirely acceptable. It should not, however, be used as a synonym for "happen" or "occur."

U

unique Something is *unique* if it is the sole existing example of its type. The word derives from the Latin *unicus*, meaning "one and only." A thing can therefore be *quite unique* or perhaps even *almost unique* ("This 1932 limousine version is almost *unique;* only three were ever made"), but it is to misuse a valuable word to say *very unique, more unique, remarkably unique,* etc.

venal, venial These two Latinate words are easily confused but should not be.

Venal means "corrupt, able to be bribed," as in "The local police were thoroughly *venal*."

Venial means "forgivable, pardonable," as in "*venial* sins."

vulnerable The word should be pronounced with four syllables and with the *l* sounded, and not as *vunn'rable*.

who, whom "The junior civil servant *whom* the government has claimed is implicated in insider dealing has been allowed to return to work at the Office of Fair Trading" (*Times*, 1988, italics added).

As this example indicates, many people have a problem with whether to use *who* or *whom* as the relative pronoun in sentences of this kind. What seems to happen is that they see *whom* as the object of a verb, in this case "has claimed," and fail to notice that this is subordinate to, in this case, "The junior civil servant *who*...is implicated in insider dealing...."

The matter becomes less confusing if we see phrases such as "the government has claimed" as parenthetic, and put imaginary brackets around them thus: "The junior civil servant *who* (the government has claimed) is implicated in insider dealing...."

The problem could be avoided altogether by using the accusative plus infinitive—"The junior civil servant *whom* the government has claimed to be implicated in insider dealing..."—but this may well be thought to be too formal for current usage.

James Cochrane

the end

About the Author

James Cochrane was born in Edinburgh in 1938 and was educated there and at Cambridge University. He joined Penguin Books as an editor in 1961 and has worked in publishing ever since. His earlier books include *Stipple, Wink and Gusset* (Century, 1992) and the *Chambers Dictionary Game Dictionary* (Chambers, 1988).